ISFJ: 33 Secrets From The Life of an ISFJ

By Diana Jackson

Contents

ISFJ: Introverted, Sensing, Feeling, Judging

1. Takes care of others

Positive: ISFJs are truly nurturing souls whose sincere compassion extends beyond just their fellow humans and also includes the creatures from the animal world. Thoughtful and enthusiastic about helping in whatever way they can, ISFJs are like comforting mothers with a plate of cookies after a long day or an all-natural remedy for whatever ails you, and they're dependable and reliable about it, too.

Negative: Their willingness to take care of others has two drawbacks: first, like all nurturers, they don't always realize when their genuine concern has crossed a line into smothering; and second, they can get so wrapped up in their care for others that they neglect themselves. ISFJs can get incredibly worn out by their devotion, which ultimately inhibits them from their cause.

In Relationships: The ISFJ partner and family might morph into the biggest babies on the planet, because their ISFJ nurturer just loves to lavish attention and care onto them. When they're sick, they can expect homemade soup, and when they're in perfect health, they can expect thoughtful gestures like a favorite meal on a bad day or a back rub for the spouse while watching their can't-miss show.

At Work: The ISFJ impulse to take care of others often directs them in their career choices, and while their feeling aspect informs their compassion, their sensing and judging aspects give them a firm, organized and dutiful practicality that doesn't just dream of helping third-world orphans, but actually propels the ISFJ into meaningful action – heading up a non-profit or serving as a nurse in war-torn countries.

2. Likes to be polite

Positive: As feelers, the ISFJ is not only deeply emotional themselves, they are attuned to others' emotions and base their actions on the expected reactions of others. Since it's always wise to err on the side of caution, this means that the ISFJ treats everyone with politeness, from the president to the homeless man begging for change. The best way to avoid offending is to mind your manners.

Negative: However, some situations call for a more pointed and direct reaction. For instance, if the ISFJ has been waiting in line at a busy department store for 15 minutes, and someone joins their friend right in front of them, effectively cutting everyone, the ISFJ is too polite to say something – when they should really speak up and stand up for themselves.

In Relationships: ISFJs slide from confrontation like true feeling types, preferring to keep the harmony than ruffle feathers. So even if the ISFJ and his/her mate is having an argument or going through a rough patch, they are going to refrain from resorting to snotty or vindictive behavior and always take the high road. Would that more people were like this!

At Work: ISFJs can come across some shady characters in their work, particularly if they venture into the social work field, but they'll always be the ones who make headway with difficult people because of their determined politeness. It's a simple act, but one that can make marginalized people feel human again, causing them to open up to the compassionate ISFJ in their lives.

3. Tends toward generosity

Positive: Donating the coat off their back to someone in need or lending a friend a few hundred dollars to tide them over until payday – these are the kinds of acts that make the ISFJ so popular and beloved among all who know them or who come into contact with them, however briefly. Their generosity is storied, and it has likely helped more than few people see the good in humanity again.

Negative: The downside to so much generosity is the ISFJ's susceptibility to manipulation and being used by people with more sinister motives. Though they are generally intelligent and capable of seeing what's in front of them, ISFJs like to give people the benefit of the doubt, and it can lead to their being burned.

In Relationships: The ISFJ partner is generous in all things: displays of affection, loving words, gifts and undivided attention. As a feeling personality, they place a high value on love and relationships, and the enamored ISFJ cannot do enough to show how much they care. If they're lucky, they will find someone who equals them in generosity, because they deserve some spoiling, too.

At Work: The ISFJ takes as much pleasure in other people's accomplishments at work as they do in their own, so coworkers of this surprisingly social introvert shouldn't be surprised if they walk by their boss's office and hear the ISFJ giving a glowing report of the teamwork and unity of the staff. Further, ISFJs are generous with their time, willing to work overtime or help coworkers.

4. Completely dependable

Positive: As mentioned, ISFJs are a dependable sort. It's partially because of their sensing aspect, which imbues them with a strong, dutiful nature to do the right thing, but their feeling aspect plays a role in it, too: ISFJs cannot bear to consider how someone would feel if they let them down or disappointed them in some way. For these reasons, the ISFJ's word is as good as gold.

Negative: Dependable people – and people like the ISFJ in particular, who try to see the good in everyone – can sometimes find that their dependability is ill-rewarded by others. Disappointment and perhaps even some anger or annoyance is common, because it is difficult for the ISFJ to imagine that other people simply aren't as reliable as they. It's a shame, because the ISFJ deserves more than they occasionally receive.

In Relationships: If their beloved partner needs a lift to and from work, despite it being 20 minutes out of their way, the ISFJ is on it. If the ISFJ promises his/her kids they will be at the soccer game that is set during a work meeting, they will find a way to be there. The ISFJ is absolutely solid when it comes to the promises they make to the people they love.

At Work: ISFJs tend to pursue careers that allow them to help others, and since helping others is close to their hearts, you can expect that this personality type will take their work very seriously – no missed deadlines, rushing to completion or under-performing here. The ISFJ would also rather have a hand cut off than be late to work, even if everyone else is rolling in casually.

5. Has a friendly, yet quiet demeanor

Positive: The ISFJ won't be the center of the attention, but if you see them at a party you will find them happily and easily chatting with a few people at a time. They are friendly and polite and always know the right thing to say, but their natural introversion leads them to seek out smaller groups. Once they are established as part of a small conversation, their positive personality aspects really shine.

Negative: The ISFJ can sometimes send mixed signals because they are both friendly and kind but somewhat reserved. People may leave a conversation feeling as though the ISFJ is a very nice and likeable person, but that they don't really know them at the same time. With a little patience, everyone can discover how great ISFJs are, but people have to be willing to stick around and dig deeper.

In Relationships: This personality dilemma goes double for the potential mates of the ISFJ, who can leave a date totally confused as to whether or not they should call again. ISFJs are the types who will say "yes" to a second date just to be nice, so to avoid hurt feelings down the road, this personality type has to be more upfront and direct about whether or not they like someone.

At Work: ISFJs are among the most sociable of the introverts, but they don't tend to show too much gregariousness at the workplace (that would be unprofessional). But with their natural affinity for helping others and showing a smiling face while doing it, this means that the quiet ISFJ is an ideal candidate for many public service careers, which require calm and composure.

6. Responsible in all aspects of their lives

Positive: As emotional personalities, the ISFJ's feeling aspect is given much-needed balance and gravitas from his/her sensing and judging aspects, both of which keep them grounded and productive. Further, ISFJs have a strong sense of duty and a talent for getting things done, which produces one highly emotionally intelligent and responsible individual. It's a really beautiful combination!

Negative: Because they feel it is their duty to be responsible for themselves and others, the ISFJ can have a difficult time carving out "me-time," which can eventually lead them to feel not a small measure of resentment toward everything that has been heaped onto their plate. For the most part, ISFJs are buoyant and resilient, hopeful optimists who look at the bright side, but everyone eventually hits a wall.

In Relationships: In relationships, ISFJs are wonderfully affectionate and loving, yet they are equally up to the tasks that make legal institutions like marriage work. They can get the bills paid, recognize and accomplish tasks like housework and home management and be counted on to provide excellent care for children and pets. In short, they are mature grown-ups who deserve to be with an equal.

At Work: ISFJs operate on the old adage that you're only on time if you're 15 minutes early. And time management is only one of the ways that this personality type knocks it out of the ballpark when it comes to their career. ISFJs don't take anything for granted, including and especially employment, and they respond by giving their all, 100 percent of the time.

7. Conscientious toward others

Positive: ISFJs are freely giving, always thinking about the comfort and needs of others. They're the perfect hosts, topping off a friend's cup of coffee during a casual hang out or ensuring that everyone has the wine of their choice at a dinner party. And this conscientiousness extends toward total strangers, as ISFJs are the type to give up their place in line at the grocery store to the mother of a squalling infant who clearly just wants to go home.

Negative: Always thinking about others is generally a positive trait, but ISFJs can become doormats if they're not careful. While they are willing to stand up for themselves if necessary, for the most part they let the rudeness of others slide, and drawing the line between action and inaction can be difficult for them – especially because they don't want to hurt anyone's feelings with an insensitive outburst.

In Relationships: ISFJs can be maddeningly selfless, a fact that can make their mates roll their eyes heavenward (though it is impossible not to appreciate the goodness that ISFJs generate wherever they go). ISFJs make the effort to keep a balance between their public and private lives, though, so that their partners and families never feel neglected as a consequence.

At Work: Coworkers love the ISFJ at their workplace, because this is the thoughtful personality who says, "Hey, Barb, I think you forgot to stick your lunch in the fridge, so I put it on the top shelf for ya." They are equally thoughtful when it comes to more professional matters, too, like scheduling around people's family responsibilities or making new employees feel welcome and included.

8. Thorough and accurate in all they do

Positive: If you need to have a job done, and it requires some sort of emphasis on empathy or compassion, you should turn to the ISFJ, who not only works hard, but completes everything they do with thoroughness and accuracy (no phonin' it in here). They can organize food drives or whip up a big Christmas dinner with all the fixings with efficiency, while keeping in mind the human reason behind what they do.

Negative: Thoroughness and accuracy – if you didn't know any better, you'd think the ISFJ held themselves up as a pillar of perfection. Well, they can tend to do so, but no one is perfect, and if they ever fail to meet their own expectations, they will take it hard and personally, and it can take a lot to get them to snap out of it.

In Relationships: Hopefully ISFJs find themselves appreciative mates, because they have so much to offer with so few drawbacks in the relationship arena. They are simply good at relationships, both from an emotional and practical standpoint, and you can bet if the ISFJ's mate likes their pancakes a certain way, they will get them that way every time.

At Work: Thanks to their judging aspect, ISFJs actually enjoy getting detail-oriented and being able to check off all the little boxes on their work to-do list. A job well done is a job completely and utterly done, with no loose strings, which is why they make such effective teachers, nurses and social workers – jobs with strong social aspects but also tons of paperwork.

9. Unafraid of displays of loyalty

Positive: If you're the person who made a total fool of himself in front of the entire school once, that person who invited you to sit with them at the cafeteria – when everyone else avoided your gaze – was probably an ISFJ. ISFJs aren't noisy crusader types, but they will always show their loyalty in small yet meaningful ways.

Negative: Not even the smallest deed will go unnoticed forever, though, and the ISFJ often leaves a trail of loyal gestures that can be traced back to them. Their willingness to do or say the right thing, in the face of a strong and unscrupulous opposition, can earn them enemies – enemies who will stoop to acts of pettiness and malice the ISFJ would consider far beneath him/herself.

In Relationships: If you need to stand up to your domineering mother, you will want your ISFJ partner by your side. When they choose a mate, they choose one for life, and it is for the ones they love that ISFJs are most willing to make the flashiest displays of their loyalty. Watch out for the ISFJ who is defending his or her own!

At Work: Whether they're standing up for a coworker who is being dumped on by everyone else or a boss who is unpopular yet always fair, the ISFJ has a way of appealing to both the emotionally driven and the logics in the crowd. They are capable of making a passionate yet well-reasoned stand that wins over majorities.

10. Kind-hearted and considerate toward others

Positive: The world seems to be lacking in kindness these days, as we bury ourselves in our technology. The ISFJ sees all this with dismay and does his or her best to get us back to basics, back to interacting with one another face-to-face and treating everyone as we would like to be treated. ISJFs go out of their way to set an example as a kind-hearted citizen.

Negative: Again, though, ISFJs also leave themselves open to manipulation or being used by people with no conscience. Though they are practical, they are emotional idealists, and when they are faced with the stunning reality of human nature – that it can be brutish and cruel – the ISFJ can end up suffering a huge existential crisis and may become embittered as a result.

In Relationships: The funny thing about ISFJs is that although they feel a great deal of emotion and have no difficulty expressing it, their practical sensing aspect influences the way they express it – so that romantic gestures include high-end pruning shears for gardening enthusiasts or a generous gift card to the spa (not chocolate and flowers). But for a certainty, their heart is always in the right place and everything they do for their families is out of love.

11. Always looks for and believes in the best in people

Positive: If there is a hopeful optimist out there, it's the ISFJ, the introvert who can withstand the most social interaction before needing to withdraw in order to recharge their batteries. As a paradoxical people-person, the ISFJ enjoys being around others because they are constantly seeing the good in them, and in turn, they give others the opportunity to see all of their special goodness.

Negative: Despite how practical ISFJs can be, they can also be incredibly naïve when it comes to seeing beneath the surface of some of the people they are helping. Despite their good intentions, it can take years in some cases for them to see people for who they really are, because they will doggedly put their faith in the knowledge that everyone must be as well-intentioned as they are.

In Relationships: ISFJs can end up in dangerous relationships if they are not careful, because a practiced manipulator can blind the ISFJ to their true, malicious intent. But in a different vein, the ISFJ is a loving and forgiving partner to those who deserve them, as they are willing to overlook the past with a hope and a prayer for a better future.

At Work: There is no more motivating coworker than the ISFJ, who can pull anyone out of their career slump by pointing out all the great things someone has going for them. ISJFs also help to keep the peace at work, because no matter how mean someone is to them, up to a very far point they keep their composure and remind themselves that even this jerk has something to offer.

12. Believes in the merits of harmony and cooperation

Positive: As an introvert who feels surprisingly at ease among company for a long period of time, the ISFJ is a great person to turn to when mediation is necessary. They themselves enjoy being called upon to help smooth over tense social situations, because they genuinely want everyone to get along and like each other. "Come on, people," the ISFJ thinks, "is it really that hard?!"

Negative: The ISFJ, who always means well, might interject their help where no one asked for it, though, and while they tried to promote harmony and cooperation among warring factions or sides, there is a chance they could just make it worse by forcing something that isn't mean to be.

In Relationships: ISFJs are such generous partners because they try not to hold a grudge. Yet they have to find and stiffen their backbones when it comes to their emphasis on relationship harmony, because with the wrong mate, they could end up finding themselves conceding more and more in the name of peace, until there is nothing good left for them.

At Work: ISFJs make such good counselors because they are not only perceptive to people's feelings, they have the practical element to offer sound advice for moving forward and past previous conflict. It's easy to see how their desire to bring harmony – and therefore happiness – into the world also makes them excellent teachers for all ages, as well as mediation lawyers.

13. Empathic and sensitive to others' feelings

Positive: Few personality types are quite so in tune with others' feelings, because as introverts, the ISFJ – without even realizing it – often spends his/her downtime considering the people they have come into contact with, long after the meeting. And you can bet they are thinking of ways they can help that person or show them some kindness to brighten their day.

Negative: Empathic people carry a double-edged sword, because while they are uniquely in-tune with how others think and feel, those feelings can overwhelm them. Depressed or grieving people can leave such an impact on the ISFJ that this personality type absorbs the negative energy as their own and carries it themselves.

In Relationships: ISFJs don't like to step on toes, not the toes of strangers or those they care about in love-match relationships. While this makes them incredibly generous and thoughtful partners, it leaves them vulnerable to an all-give, no-receive arrangement, where their own feelings take a back seat to the needs of their loved ones.

At Work: As coworkers, ISFJs would be the last people to make a rude comment in a flash of anger – that is just not their style, and others count on their kindness. As an aid worker or service-based employee, ISFJs shine when they are in the position to help others, because their empathic natures allow them to make real, deep connections.

14. Values security

Positive: As sensing personalities who value practicality and tradition, ISFJs appreciate being able to put down roots, whether it's a house or an established friendship of decades. When they are able to attain security in their lives, ISFJs themselves become more secure and confident people, which makes them much more effective in all other aspects of their lives.

Negative: In contrast, if they cannot attain security, ISFJs can become less confident and perhaps even more susceptible to the malicious designs of others. For instance, a homeowner who is selling might get a whiff of the ISFJ's obvious desperation to purchase their dream home, and could take advantage by negotiating a higher price.

In Relationships: There is no doubt about it: ISFJs are settlers. Not in the sense that they will settle for anything or anyone – not by a long shot – but in that they desire a traditional home setting, house, spouse, children, maybe even a few pets. They don't mind the idea of growing old with someone.

At Work: ISFJs might be able to work as freelancers, but they'd be looking for full-time employment the whole time. ISFJs naturally desire traditional careers that come with the works: 40-hour work weeks, paid vacation, holidays off, sick days and benefits. They don't want to hop from career to career – they want to find the job where they are committed for decades.

15. Holds kindness in the highest regard

Positive: Kindness has been pushed to the wayside in today's modern society, as people's greed continues to grow and grow. Luckily, ISFJs have always kept their feet on the ground and remembered what's important: being good to one another, even if it doesn't make you rich or famous. Thank goodness for ISFJs, because without their kindness the world be a much darker and less hospitable place to live.

Negative: About 95 percent of the situations we face each day would be improved with kindness, but the world is a hard place – no amount of smiling can make that untrue – and in some situations, toughness would be more effective. The ISFJ can turn the other cheek again and again when it comes to bullies, but sometimes the only anecdote is to stand up for oneself right away.

In Relationships: If they can help it, ISFJs will hold in the sharp comments and the nasty comebacks. They'll refrain as much as possible from taking out their bad day on their partners and families. As far as they are concerned, love is kindness, and giving into those sarcastic or snippy impulses is to be avoided at all costs.

At Work: ISFJs tend to be beloved in their places of work, respected for their committed work ethic but also truly cared about because they show everyone kindness, from the stressed out boss at the top of the work hierarchy to the janitor who sweeps up at the end of the day. In fact, the ISFJ remembers the birthday for both and gifts them equally, considering them more than just work colleagues.

16. Modest about self

Positive: There are enough people out there pushing themselves forward and demanding attention and adulation. ISFJs deserve as much recognition as anyone for the work they do, but you wouldn't think it to talk to them. Part of their incomparable charm is their endearing modesty – they blush every time as if your compliment means more than anything else they have ever heard.

Negative: Modesty can be taken to extremes, and ISFJs are susceptible to having other people take credit for their work, simply because they won't stand up and say, "Yes, that was me. I did this." Because they tend to credit "the team effort," they leave the door wide open for a dishonest, conniving opportunist with no scruples to announce that it was all them.

In Relationships: ISFJ mates know how great they have it, and if they're any sort of decent guy or gal, they'll tell their partner all the time – though it doesn't matter, because ISFJs will always blush and say, "Oh, you exaggerate." The thing is, ISFJs might not be perfect (who is?) but they do relationships very well.

At Work: Work is the place where ISFJs could really find themselves screwed over by a coworker with less-than-honorable integrity. What's worse, they would never find out unless someone said something to them, because as far as they are concerned, no one would ever do something so dishonest. ISFJs have to learn to take credit when they have done a good job!

17. Avoids confrontation if possible

Positive: What all reality TV stars have in common is that they charge toward conflict like a beagle on the hunt. This could be very entertaining for ISFJs, but they would never want that much drama in their own lives. This personality type just wants everyone to get along – is that so hard?

Negative: Keeping the peace is one thing, but ISFJs have a tendency to avoid confrontation for so long that it only ends up turning into a bigger and bigger conflict, as the other party gets angrier that they are being ignored and avoided. ISFJs have to learn to face their adversaries and resolve arguments effectively, even if it's reaching out with an email or text.

In Relationships: In relationships especially ISFJs have to learn that it's okay for both parties to be upset. What matters more is how they resolve their differences and move forward. Avoiding confrontation only makes problems worse; hopefully ISFJs learn this and adjust their responses to conflict accordingly.

At Work: ISFJs aren't interesting in squabbling with their coworkers, and if someone has a problem with them, they tend to just try and keep out of that person's way. This only exacerbates the situation. As in the other aspects of their lives, ISFJs must try instead to achieve harmony and peace by working things out, not avoiding them.

18. Has deep respect for laws and traditions

Positive: The laws and traditions which keep our families and especially our children safe are the ones that the nurturing ISFJ values most. These aren't dreamy idealists, hoping for a better tomorrow; these are the people who are sometimes on the front lines in our communities, not only upholding laws and traditions, but teaching them to the next generation.

Negative: Sometimes laws have been around for so long that they are no longer relevant. Sometimes traditions can get it wrong. ISFJs are good people whose belief and faith in what they have always known to be true can sometimes cause them to be exclusionary, close-minded and blind to reality.

In Relationships: Like the ISTJ, ISFJs want that "American Dream" family life, with a spouse, children and a beautiful home. Gender roles may be more strictly defined and assigned according to tradition (men at work, women at home), and ISFJs will try to pass on their good old-fashioned values to the kids – though whether or not they take remains to be seen.

At Work: ISFJs thrive in work situations where their roles are clearly defined – they know what their job is, everyone else knows the same, and people stay on task (nothing could bother an ISFJ more than when a coworker unceremoniously dumps their work load on him/her without even the manners to say "Hey, is it okay?"). ISFJs are sticklers for rules as much as good etiquette.

19. Inflexible, resistant to change

Positive: Sometimes, it seems like people want to change things just for the sake of mixing things up, when the original person, place or thing was absolutely fine to begin with. It's a simple matter of leaving well enough alone, and the ISFJ is a strong proponent. If you can't show them any practical or reasonable reason, they will remain unconvinced (and rightly so).

Negative: When the civil rights movement swept across the United States in the 1960s, certain people stubbornly stood on the wrong side of history. In today's social climate, the blacks, women and gays continue to fight for equal rights, for the turning of the tide, yet still meet with resistance. ISFJs are heartfelt, deeply giving people, but sometimes their values can be old-fashioned and they can be unwilling to change.

In Relationships: Hopefully, when it comes to change, the ISFJ's partner has a good sense of humor and a whole lot of patience. This personality type will eventually come 'round, whether it's a fresh coat of paint in the living room or an entirely new city, but they'll drag their feet a bit as they slowly get accustomed and start to see all the new good that surrounds them.

At Work: Go ahead and try to change the desk arrangement with a group of ISFJs – we dare you. This normally cheerful and smiling bunch will turn into a ferocious pack of bone-crunching hyenas. Ultimately, if the change makes sense – if it makes things easier for everyone – the ISFJ will end up embracing the difference, but they must be convinced.

20. Able to learn best while performing hands-on tasks

Positive: A lot of people quake at the idea of hitting the ground running, but because of their strong sensing aspect, ISFJs prefer to learn by doing, and they are quick studies whose hands and minds easily grasp the concepts they are being taught. This often means that they are incredibly talented in a short time when it comes to ornate craft making, building with all manner of materials, and even teaching others in this fashion.

Negative: This could possibly mean that ISFJs weren't or aren't the best classroom students. Subjects like the core math, science, history and English require learning by thinking through complex ideas and concepts. That can be difficult for the ISFJ, who just want something tangible that they can see and touch. Luckily, ISFJs supplement their middling grades with a can-do attitude.

In Relationships: ISFJs can spend a lot of time helping others with their various types of relationships, but when it comes to their own, they aren't sure what path they would take or word they would speak until they are there, in the moment, with their partner facing them and expecting some kind of response. It is possible to improve at being in a relationship, and the ISFJ does so with every partner.

At Work: ISFJs are often in careers where they do a lot of public good, like nursing or teaching. These are the types of jobs where they do more than just sit around and think about what's possible – they live what is possible in the world, every day. And because of how they themselves learn, this makes them excellent trainers and advisors to new recruits in their field.

21. Values practical applications

Positive: Sensing ISFJs might not get the credit for wild theories and predictions like their intuitive counterparts, but that doesn't mean they aren't creative. For example, ISFJs could run Pinterest, because these personality types of chock full of ideas for how simple, everyday items can be repurposed for some incredibly helpful, practical and convenient uses. That's just how they roll.

Negative: ISFJs were the little rebels in middle school who thought (but didn't say, because they were too well brought up to make such a rude comment out loud), "When am I ever going to need algebra outside of this class?" If it's a skill or a nugget of knowledge that they can't see themselves using every day, they'd just rather not. But life has a surprising way of coming full circle, and ISFJs can find themselves unprepared.

In Relationships: As practical sensing types and deeply committed, caring human beings, ISFJs are the first ones to consult a book or a therapist if there is a problem in their relationship. They want advice, advice that can be applied, used and which will generate tangible results. It is so like the ISFJ to go into problem-solving mode, even when it comes to their feelings.

At Work: If they were thinking types, they'd be happier in the sciences, but as feeling types, ISFJs have a strong desire to work with people in a way that is hands-on, face-to-face. They want to help people learn and resolve conflict, and they seek to do this by offering real guidance, practical advice has been proven by experts and can be seen to work again and again.

22. Extremely dependable, trustworthy and reliable

Positive: Dependability, trustworthiness and reliability? It's like ISFJs have hit the personality jackpot, because these three traits ensure that people are well-liked, with a wide range of friends and acquaintances; it ensures that they are well-employed; and it enables them to have a happy and healthy home life.

Negative: The downside to these traits is that ISFJs can often find that people expect quite a bit out of them, and may even begin to take them for granted. It's not a far reach for someone to ask their ISFJ friend to watch her kids for a few hours once in a while, and then gradually ask again and again, until the ISFJ is practically an unpaid nanny.

In Relationships: As mentioned, ISFJs have their faults, but they are extremely good at relationships, and part of the reason is because they can be relied upon so readily. They are simply the kinds of people with whom you want to settle down, because they are nurturers, providers and exceptionally loving and giving parents.

At Work: In places of work where people can be demonstrably irresponsible and untrustworthy – looking at you, schools filled with teenagers or therapists' offices full of neurotics – the ISFJ is a shining beacon of hope, the glue that holds things together in the midst of all the chaos. In a lot of cases they go unappreciated, because they would be the first to protest that they are just doing their job.

23. Has a well-developed sense of space, function and aesthetic appeal

Positive: There is a certain harmony to everything in the ISFJ's immediate environment, and that's not a coincidence. Their sensing aspect is like a gauge which measures good taste and practicality – artistic ISFJs especially benefit from this part of their personality, particularly those who do commercial work like jewelry-making or interior design. But you can see it even in their cars or their workspaces.

Negative: It can be difficult for ISFJs to divorce themselves from their desire to find a use and a reason for every object in their lives. Sometimes things exist just for fun or to be silly, and while everyone else is having a laugh, ISFJs are standing there scratching their heads, thinking, "I just don't get it." If they aren't careful, their dismay can show on their faces and may even offend some.

In Relationships: If you want to have a beautiful home that is neat, organized and yet feels like people actually live there, marry an ISFJ, who has a knack for decorating in ways that are pleasing to the eye, while actually affording the residents a great deal of convenience. They're the type with a perfectly organized spice rack that's also a one-of-a-kind hand-made piece they found on Etsy.

At Work: ISFJs might not be easy with profound change in the workplace, but they would certainly embrace an office facelift, and they'll have plenty of ideas for sprucing up the place, while also making everything more accessible. ISFJs will bring the naturally air filtering plants that look good beautiful but also serve a purpose.

24. Cognizant of their own feelings

Positive: There are a lot of people out there who cannot decide how they feel. About anything! But as both feeling and judging types, ISFJs know emotion and they can make decisions, allowing them to easily pinpoint how they feel about something so that their practicality can take over and move them forward toward resolution. ISFJs are like well-oiled emotion machines.

Negative: Nothing scares people off like someone with self-confidence and poise. While this is most definitely other people's problems, ISFJs can be weirdly intimidating, because when one is cognizant of and honest with their feelings, they have a better sense of self than those who don't. And that can really make less sure individuals back away or even react with hostility.

In Relationships: ISFJs are fortunate that they don't always have to talk, talk, talk about their feelings – just being able to recognize them is good enough, but if their partner is open to big, emotional discussions, then all the better! This can give couples an incredible advantage, because communication is undoubtedly the key to relationship bliss.

At Work: If an ISFJ has an outburst on-the-job, you know something bad happened. Otherwise, this feelings-based yet practical personality type has the emotional intelligence to recognize what they are experience – be it anger, betrayal or whatever – and then figure out how to get over it and move it without creating a scene or drumming up unnecessary drama.

25. Able to help others become aware of their own feelings

Positive: If you have ever had a friend listen to you while you blathered on about some problem in your life, and then they responded with an absolutely precise, hit-the-nail-on-the-head assessment of how you are feeling, then perhaps that friend was an ISFJ. This personality type excels when it comes to listening and assessing.

Negative: On the flipside, sometimes we vent and that's all we really want or need at the moment. The ISFJ almost can't help him or herself – they want to help, and with the best of intentions. But for those moments when someone just needs to get something off their chest without taking it any further, the ISFJ "this is how things are" assessment can be a real annoyance.

In Relationships: Less emotionally intelligent types – looking at you, thinkers – who are open to the idea that they can learn to recognize their feelings and then adjust their behavior so that it is more productive and fitting with the situation can benefit from having an ISFJ partner. In turn, it is good for the ISFJ to learn that not everyone is as in-tune with their emotions as they.

At Work: ISFJs make extraordinary therapists, psychologists, psychiatrists, guidance counselors and other mental health professionals, because the whole point of the field is to help others recognize and get in touch with their emotional states and decide how to move forward and grow with that knowledge.

26. Always sees tasks through to completion

Positive: Responsible and resolute, the ISFJ can be counted upon to finish what they start. They are deeply committed to the idea of commitment itself, and if they feel that others are counting on them to complete something, well, all the more reason they cannot let the project go unfinished – their sense of duty simply won't allow it.

Negative: ISFJs can have tunnel vision when they feel it is their mission to do something, even if the circumstances around the mission change. Some might call it steadiness, but in a lot of ways, it's just good old-fashioned stubbornness, so that even when the situation changes and the project should be abandoned, the ISFJ plods, futilely, forward.

In Relationships: At least in their home life, ISFJs are model DIYers who would never leave a room half-painted or a chair partially un-sanded. They are also emotionally committed, so that their partners know they can be counted upon to show up on time, exactly when they said they would.

At Work: ISFJs are an employer's dream to have around the workplace, because this is the type of personality who will stay late, even when everyone else has gone home, including the janitors, to finish an important report or slideshow for the next day. ISFJs may also encourage their coworkers to follow suit, improving overall workplace output.

27. Absolutely trustworthy in all situations

Positive: Even if the secret goes against everything the ISFJ believes in, you can bet that if they have given their word not to tell, their lips are sealed. This makes them extraordinarily prized confidants and friends, and their discretion can get them far in life, because everyone wants to be around someone they can trust.

Negative: ISFJs are sought-after because of their trustworthiness, but without, say, the religious protection of a priest (whose confessions are absolutely unrepeatable) the ISFJ is not bound to a higher power and should therefore not feel as though secrets which are detrimental to the safety or health of others must be kept. But the black-and-white morality of the ISFJ might hold firm regardless, causing calamity.

In Relationships: Despite having "judging" in their personality type – although the word has a different meaning – ISFJs are actually surprisingly open-minded and they do, in particular, recognize the importance of open lines of communication with their significant others. Because their trustworthiness is proven, they may enjoy total and enviable frankness with their mates.

At Work: Being discreet and reliable in the workplace is a good recipe for promotion. ISFJs prove themselves again and again to be the employee who can be relied upon for anything, whether it's plugging in those extra hours or just being on time the day after the Super Bowl. It's the little things that add up when someone is due for a raise.

28. Can be awkward in social situations

Positive: There is something incredibly endearing about someone who isn't quite, 100 percent sure of themselves in mixed company. They blush when they talk or fidget by twirling hair or biting their lip, and it's kind of adorable to everyone present. So the ISFJ is a little awkward in groups – they have more than enough thoughtfulness and kindness to make up for it!

Negative: As deeply giving and concerned individuals, however, ISFJs often feel the urge to be among people, helping them directly, face-to-face. Their awkwardness can be interpreted as something other, like aloofness or just all-around strangeness, and it can be off-putting to the people they are trying to bring aid to.

In Relationships: ISFJs will dutifully attend their significant others' social engagements, such as work functions or nights out with their friends, but they'll probably be yearning for home (and it might show on their faces). Still, it helps to practice – the more ISFJs go out there and practice being sociable, the better and the easier it will get.

At Work: ISFJs might start off awkward at work, but they have a real talent for picking careers at which they are prone to succeed, so their confidence will build as the months go by. Sure, the Christmas party might be a little difficult for them, what with all the spouses they don't know, but on any given Monday, they'll sail through the day with a shining confidence.

29. Has trouble saying no to others

Positive: "Yes" is something ISFJs say more often than not, because they just can't help themselves – they want to help out and make others' jobs easier. It's part of what makes them so popular, because they not only agree to lend a hand, they actually show up and then work really hard.

Negative: ISFJs can find themselves with a full plate – indeed, a plate where the food is starting to fall off the sides to the ground. ISFJs have to learn how to decline once in a while, or they are going to end up slaves to anyone who comes up to them and asks for a moment, just a moment, of their time. (Note to ISFJs: it's never just a moment.)

In Relationships: ISFJs can run into problems where they end up on dates with people they have zero attraction to. This is because the personality type is just a giving, charitable sort. Yet the ISFJ's charity is someone else's "first step toward marriage with the perfect man/woman." Better to just learn how to let someone down gently.

At Work: With any luck the ISFJ ends up with a boss who displays integrity and restraint, otherwise they will end up at the beck and call of the authority figure who doles out the workloads – and the promotions. If pushed too far, ISFJs will eventually be forced to find their voice and learn the courage to say "no."

30. Thrives on positive feedback

Positive: Everyone likes to hear that they have done a good job, but none so much as the ISFJ, who actually takes the compliments that they receive and uses them as fuel for the fire. Positive feedback inspires the ISFJ to keep on doing what they're doing or even to take their efforts to the next level.

Negative: Not all feedback in life is positive, of course, and so ISFJs have to learn to withstand critique as graciously as they accept praise. It can be difficult, though, because critique sounds a lot like criticism, and ISFJs don't want to hear how they were doing something wrong. Still, it's the only way to learn anything.

In Relationships: If you like your ISFJ partner's cooking, then tell him or her. If you think the way they fold laundry is exception, say so. Nothing could make the ISFJ happier than knowing that they are doing a good job and are pleasing their mates – and nothing works better to keep them interested in helping with chores than praise.

At Work: ISFJs can get by without a constant stream of praise in the workplace, but you have to throw them a bone once in a while and let them know they're doing a good job, or else they're bound to get disenchanted and discouraged – they might even consider quitting and going somewhere where the positive feedback flows more readily.

31. Can become easily discouraged at criticism

Positive: Discouragement isn't great, but if there was ever a way to get the ISFJ to change tack and try another course, criticizing the job that they've done so far is the way forward. It might cause them a deal of dismay, but going on to suggest another option is just the lead they need to forget about their past disappointment and move forward.

Negative: If you're lucky the ISFJ will simply put the past behind them, but more often than not, they'll be tempted to quit whatever endeavor they were pursuing and perhaps wallow in their disappointment and sadness for a bit. It's a touch self-indulgent, especially when other people are perfectly okay accepting criticism with thick skin.

In Relationships: And the easiest way to get your ISFJ partner to never want to pick up a pot or pan again is to tell them that their dish was on the salty side. It's not fair, of course, that you have to wear kid gloves when dealing with your sensitive introverted mate, but when they go out of their way to do so much to make you happy, well...couching your words a bit isn't so bad.

At Work: ISFJs really just need to develop thicker skin, because while their loved ones and friends are willing to go easy on them, no one at work is obligated to do so, unless of course, they are such an essential part of the workplace that no one could get on without them. Since that's a rare situation, the answer lies with the ISFJ; they have to learn how not to take things personally.

32. Can become depressed without encouragement

Positive: While it is possible for ISFJs to become depressed without some form of encouragement, it's entirely rare and not something that happens easily or overnight. It takes years of neglect for the ISFJ to develop true clinical depression, so on the plus side, with most ISFJs there is little likelihood that it will ever happen.

Negative: In the most extraordinary of situations, however, if the ISFJ has been dealt a terrible hand in life and has all but withdrawn from the world due to something like a prolonged sickness, the lack of social stimulation, affection and words of encouragement from people they know and trust can plunge them into depression, the sort that can take years to develop and years to treat.

In Relationships: If the ISFJ is in a relationship, then at least they have one person who cares for them. What's more, that person might have to be the one who gets the ISFJ to admit that something is very wrong with them and that they need professional help. With their mate's love and encouragement, though, the ISFJ can bounce back from anything.

At Work: Work might be the starting place for the ISFJ's descent into depression, especially if they majorly flubbed on a big project or if they were even fired. Since the workplace affords so many opportunities to be complimented, it helps if the ISFJ is always employed, or at least doesn't suffer stretches of unemployment for too long.

33. Shies away from being the center of attention

Positive: Like a true introvert, ISFJs might be able to mingle in small parties of company, but if all the attention were to turn to them, they'd immediately look for the nearest exit. And there's nothing wrong with that! In a society that has become increasingly self-centered, it's nice that there are still people who exhibit modesty.

Negative: There are definitely times when the ISFJ needs to stand up and take a bow, accept the attention that they so rightfully deserve and make a little spectacle out of themselves. Too many people hog the spotlight and are undeserving, but the ISFJ is an accomplished and worthy individual who does everyone a disservice by refusing to be recognized.

In Relationships: Not just in public, but at home and in private does the ISFJ shy away from being the center of attention. They would much rather put the focus on their partner or even their children. But ISFJs have to remember that especially around their loved ones, for whom they do so much, they deserve a special moment in the spotlight now and then.

At Work: Like other introverted types, the ISFJ is in danger of having someone else take credit for their work. Their unwillingness to be recognized publically could also cause them to be forgotten or ignored, especially if the "higher ups" who don't work in and around them come to visit. ISFJs should learn just a little bit of ruthlessness (or cleverness) to float by among sharks.

www.ingramcontent.com/pod-product-compliance
Lightning Source LLC
Chambersburg PA
CBHW070501290526
45790CB00003B/1053